Piranha

Other titles in the Nature's Predators series include:

- Alligators
- Carnivorous Plants
- Cheetahs
- Coyotes
- Eagles
- Fire Ants
- Grizzly Bears
- Killer Whales
- Komodo Dragons
- Lions
- Polar Bears
- Rattlesnakes
- Scorpions
- Sharks
- Snakes
- Spiders
- Tigers
- Wolves

Piranha

Rachel Lynette

**KIDHAVEN
PRESS**™

THOMSON
————— ✴ ————— ™
GALE

San Diego • Detroit • New York • San Francisco • Cleveland
New Haven, Conn. • Waterville, Maine • London • Munich

LIBRARY OF CONGRESS CATALOGING-IN-PUBLICATION DATA

Lynette, Rachel
  Piranha / by Lynette, Rachel
    v. cm. — (Nature's Predators)
  Includes bibliographical references (p.   ).
  Summary: Discusses Piranha anatomy, behavior, hunting practices, diet, habitat, and threats they face from humans.
    ISBN 0-7377-1888-9 (hardback : alk. paper)
  1. Piranha—Juvenile literature. I. Title. II. Series.
  QL638.C507 2004
  597'.48—dc21

                                                                    2003008277

Printed in the United States of America

CONTENTS

CHAPTER ONE

The Legendary Piranha: Evil in the Amazon

An injured **capybara** comes to a shallow watering hole to drink and to soothe its infected wound in the cool water. All seems quiet. Suddenly, it is bitten in one leg, then another. Within seconds over twenty olive-sized bites have been torn from its body. Still conscious, it collapses into the water, which is now tinted red with blood and teeming with small fish. The attackers become even more vicious, making a hole in the capybara's side and then swimming inside to devour its internal organs. Within minutes the capybara is reduced to a carcass of bones. The school of piranha vanishes into the weeds in search of its next meal.

The Killer Fish

The reputation of piranha as cold-blooded killers is legendary. They strike, seemingly without warning. They can eat an animal so fast that the victim may still be conscious and breathing while most of its body is already being digested by its attackers. Theodore Roosevelt, a past president of the United States, wrote of them:

> They are the most ferocious fish in the world. Even the most formidable fish, the sharks or the barracudas, usually attack things smaller than them-

---

Piranha attack without warning and devour their victims within minutes.

South American Indians fish, bathe, and swim in waters where piranha live. Knowing the habits of piranha helps the Indians avoid attack.

selves. But the piranha habitually attack things much larger than themselves. They will snap a finger off a hand incautiously trailed in the water; they mutilate swimmers—in every river town in Paraguay there are men who have been thus mutilated; they will rend and devour alive any wounded man or beast; for blood in the water excites them to madness. [1]

Yet the native Indians of Venezuela, Brazil, and other South American countries bathe and swim in waters infested with piranha every day without injury. For them the piranha are just one of many dangers in the rain forest. They know that piranha, like most animals, will attack people only under certain circumstances. Piranha are attracted to blood and may attack a person who is injured or has an open sore. Piranha will also attack almost anything when they are starving or when a lot of them are confined in a small space. In addition, piranha are attracted to splashing. Although most piranha prefer to avoid humans as prey, they might accidentally bite a human who is near the site of a piranha kill. Most native Indians consider being bitten by a piranha to be a sign of human carelessness rather than evidence of the evilness of the piranha. By knowing when and where piranha are likely to attack, the people of South America can usually live peacefully with these dangerous fish.

At Home in the Amazon

Piranha are freshwater tropical fish and can be found in rivers, streams, lagoons, and lakes throughout South America. Piranha make their homes in every major river in South America, including the Amazon, the second largest river in the world. Piranha can also be found in the Orinoco, Essequibo, de la Plata, and São Francisco Rivers. They are so common that in the Amazon basin twenty-four different towns, villages, and natural features have been named after them. They are sensitive to temperature, however, and cannot live in streams or lakes that are fed by mountain runoff because the water is too cold.

Some species of piranha swim alone, but most live together in schools of twenty to thirty fish, though some schools can have as many as three hundred.

Major Rivers of South America

VENEZUELA

GUYANA
Georgetown

SURINAME
Paramaribo

Caracas

Orinoco River

Essequibo River

FRENCH GUIANA
Cayenne

Bogotá

COLOMBIA

Amazon River

Quito
ECUADOR

PERU

BRAZIL

Lima

São Francisco River

La Paz

Brasília

BOLIVIA

Pacific
Ocean

PARAGUAY
Asunción

Atlantic
Ocean

CHILE

Santiago

URUGUAY

Buenos Aires

Montevideo

ARGENTINA

Rio de la
Plata

Several different species may live in one area, sometimes feeding on the same prey or even on each other.

Piranha Species

Scientists have identified about thirty different species of piranha. Piranha are part of a larger family of fish called Characidae. All members of the Characidae family have teeth, good hearing, and a small fleshy fin near the tail called the adipose fin. This fin stores fat in times when food is scarce. Piranha have five different fins and strong, slender tails, which allow them to lunge through the water to quickly attack their prey.

The red-bellied piranha is the most well known of the species. They are common throughout the lakes and rivers of South America. When people talk about the viciousness of piranha, it is usually the red-bellied ones they are referring too. They are in fact responsible for most of the human injuries that have been reported. As the name suggests, they have bright red bellies. They also have red throats. The rest of their bodies are greenish gray, silver, and brown. They grow to be about a foot long.

Size and Coloring

One of the most surprising things about piranha is their small size. Piranha range in size from just eight inches to nearly two feet. Most piranha are about ten to fourteen inches long. Even the São Francisco piranha, which are the largest piranha, are much smaller than many of the animals they prey on. The piranha's small size makes it possible for many piranha to crowd together and feed on a single, large animal.

Colors also vary. Most adult piranha are dark gray or olive colored, with large, dark spots on their backs and sides. This coloring helps them to blend in with their environment while waiting for prey to approach. Some species have bright red or orange bellies and black or yellow markings. Fins are often brightly colored with dark edges. The piranha's coloring changes

The red-bellied piranha, common throughout South America, is the best-known piranha species.

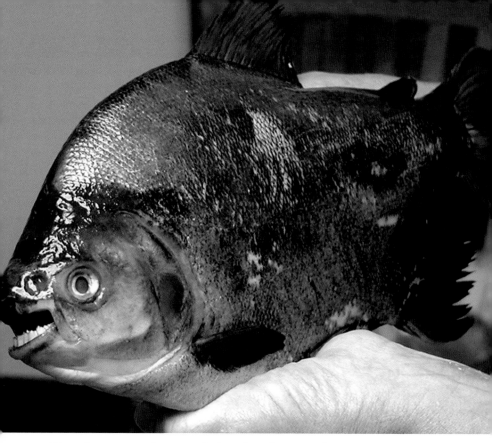

Piranha come in a variety of colors and can grow up to two feet long.

throughout its life. Young piranha are usually lighter in color and often do not have spots. The coloring on a breeding piranha is brighter in order to attract a mate.

Reproduction

Like most fish, piranha are egg-layers. Piranha **spawn** during the early part of the rainy season. Most species of piranha are nest builders. They prefer to lay their eggs in lagoons or very slow moving rivers. They make their nests by hollowing out a shallow bowl-shaped hole. Some species use leaves from floating plants to make their nests. Other piranha do not make nests. They are scatterers. The eggs they lay are sticky so that they can adhere to the weeds that grow in the water. Sometimes the weeds break off from the plant, carrying the eggs down the river. This helps to spread the species to new areas.

Females lay from seven hundred to four thousand eggs at a time, depending on the species. The male ferociously guards the eggs and the new hatchlings. Often, the female helps. The eggs hatch in about four days. The parents continue to protect the tiny newborn fish, which are called **fry**.

When fry first emerge from their eggs they are very small and blind. They stay hidden among the weeds, eating the remains of their yolk sacs for the first few days of their lives. After about a week their eyes develop enough for them to see. Scales appear soon after birth along with sharp teeth. Piranha grow quickly during the first few months of their lives. Before long they are eating seeds, fruit, insects, and then small fish.

Even very young piranha are aggressive hunters. They nip at each other and will strike at any prey that comes within their range. As they grow they become even more aggressive and can target bigger prey.

CHAPTER TWO

Built to Kill: The Anatomy and Diet of Piranha

Piranha have evolved into extremely successful hunters. Piranha have sharp senses, which they rely on to find their prey. Once they find their prey, they use both speed and cunning to make the kill. Their bodies are suited for swift, sudden attacks and for devouring their victims quickly.

Flat Bodies and Sharp Teeth

The piranha's body is built to be quick over short distances. This helps the piranha, not only when hunting, but also while feeding. The piranha is able to dodge among the other members of the school in order to get a fair share of the kill. Piranha have a flat, round body, much like a dinner plate. They have slime-producing glands under their scales. This slime covers the piranha's body, protecting it from disease and helping it to slip quickly through the water. Although the piranha is known for its swift attack, it is the muscular jaws and the teeth within them that have made the piranha the most feared fish in the world.

The piranha's jaws are extremely strong. They can tear through tough animal hides. Larger species can even bite through bones. The piranha's lower jaw sticks out farther than the upper jaw, giving the fish a bulldog appearance. This allows the piranha to take bigger bites from its victims than fish with ordinary jaws.

The piranha's lower jaw sticks out farther than the upper jaw, allowing it to take big bites of prey.

The piranha's teeth make it easy for the fish to tear chunks of flesh out of almost anything it might encounter. Piranha have flat, triangle-shaped teeth with sharp points. The edges are razor sharp. The teeth on the piranha's top jaw interlock perfectly with the spaces between the teeth on the bottom jaw. When a piranha loses a tooth it is quickly replaced by another tooth which is already fully grown in the gums.

Piranha do not chew their food. They take a bite and swallow it immediately. This allows the piranha to take many bites in a small amount of time. This is essential when food is scarce and the piranha must compete with other fish to stay alive.

Sensing Prey

The piranha's senses are essential in the hunt. Piranha have excellent eyesight. Their eyes are relatively large and they have a wide field of vision. They can see prey to the sides as well as in front of them. They see things that are close especially well, which helps them determine if a potential source of food is weak or sick. Scientists believe that piranha can see at least twenty different colors, which may help the piranha distinguish prey from their own species.

In addition to good eyesight, piranha have a keen sense of smell. They are especially sensitive to the smell of blood. Scientists have done experiments that show a piranha can smell a single drop of blood in over fifty gallons of water. This strong sense of smell helps the piranha locate injured animals, even when they are very far away.

Piranha have excellent eyesight, and a wide field of vision. They can see prey to the sides and in front of them.

The piranha's well-developed sense of hearing is also important for finding food. The first four vertebrae of a piranha's backbone are like the bones in a human's middle ear. These bones are called the **Weberian apparatus**. They use vibrations to greatly enhance the piranha's hearing. Piranha can hear high-pitched sounds especially well. Good hearing helps the piranha to detect the splashing that occurs when a large animal falls into the water, as well as the smaller splashes that attacking piranha make during a feeding frenzy.

Sensing water vibrations is another way that piranha find prey. Piranha have a special sense organ along their sides called the **lateral line**. The lateral line senses vibrations in the water, which allows the piranha to recognize both predators and prey. It can be used to detect sick fish and to navigate in rough waters where visibility is poor.

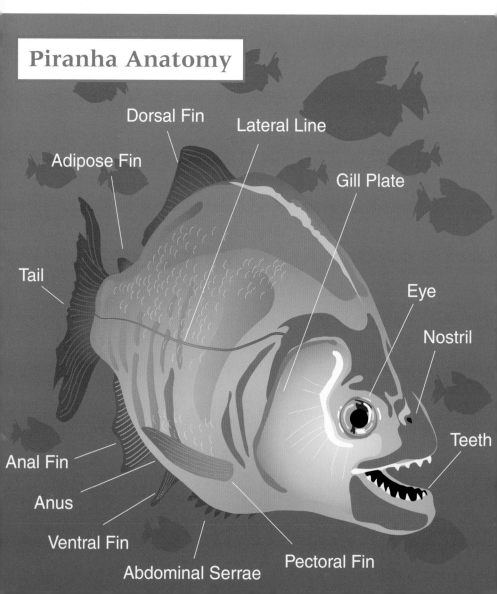

Piranha Anatomy

Dorsal Fin

Lateral Line

Adipose Fin

Gill Plate

Tail

Eye

Nostril

Teeth

Anal Fin

Anus

Ventral Fin

Pectoral Fin

Abdominal Serrae

A piranha gulps down a fish. Piranha will eat just about anything, but other fish are their most common prey.

The Piranha's Surprising Diet

Piranha are both predators and **scavengers**. When they prey on animals that are still alive, they usually choose the weak ones. If the animal is injured the smell of blood will attract the piranha. Piranha can also eat sick and even dead animals without getting sick themselves. By eating sick and dead animals, piranha fill an important role in the **ecosystem** of the Amazon basin. Piranha eat sick fish before they can spread disease to other fish and animals. By eating dead animals, piranha keep the waters clean.

Until recently, most people thought that piranha were **carnivores**. However, scientists have now found that many species are **omnivores**, eating fruit and seeds that fall in the water as well as flesh of other fish and animals. The piranha's strong teeth can bite through a hard seed as easily as it can tear off a chunk of flesh.

In addition to fruit and seeds, piranha also eat insects, shellfish, frogs, birds, rodents and other mammals, reptiles, and other fish, including other species of piranha. Usually, other fish are the most available source of food and therefore the most common prey.

Hunting Groups

Most species of piranha hunt in large schools called **shoals**. Scientists have observed that although piranha work together in the hunt, members of piranha shoals appear to be nervous and wary of each other. They watch the other fish around them carefully and avoid swimming too close to other fish or allowing other fish to swim directly behind them. A piranha that comes too close to another piranha will be aggressively chased away. This is probably because piranha will eat one of their own kind, especially if the fish seems weak, sick, or injured. One of the names natives have for the piranha, *caribe,* means cannibal.

Since piranha will sometimes eat each other, younger piranha are constantly in danger of being eaten by older and bigger piranha. This is probably why younger piranha do not form shoals with older ones. They form shoals of their own, hunting during the middle of the day and hiding in the weeds in the mornings and late afternoons when the older and bigger piranha hunt.

CHAPTER THREE

Time to Eat: When Piranha Attack

Piranha spend most of the daytime hours hunting for food. This may involve swimming long distances or simply hiding in the weeds to wait. Piranha are excellent judges of potential prey. They often choose fish that are involved in some other activity such as eating, courting, or fighting, making it less likely that the piranha will be noticed as they approach. Once they catch their food, eating it is a relatively quick affair.

Hunting Strategies

Piranha use several strategies for hunting. Since piranha can swim fast only for short distances, they have developed strategies that require only a short chase, or in some cases, no chase at all. If the first attack fails, they will rarely pursue their prey further.

Piranha often hunt together in groups called shoals. Piranha in a shoal work together to attack and devour prey.

One of the most common strategies is the **ambush**. To ambush another fish, the piranha hides in the weeds or behind a rock. When a fish approaches its hiding place, the piranha attacks quickly, surprising the other fish. By the time the prey realizes it is being attacked, it has already been bitten several times and may be too injured to fight back or swim away. This approach works especially well for small schools or lone fish.

Another common hunting method is for one member of the shoal to charge at a school of smaller fish, scattering them in all directions. Each of the piranha in the shoal then picks out a specific fleeing fish to chase. Piranha that fail to catch their own fish may be able to share with the more successful members of the shoal, but if the fish are small they will be eaten quickly and the unsuccessful piranha will have to wait for the next hunt.

Piranha that hunt alone may fool their prey into thinking they are not hunting at all. The piranha will linger around its prey starting far enough away not to alarm the fish. Pretending not to be interested in the prey, it will slowly get closer to the fish. When it gets close enough to strike, it lunges quickly, taking a bite out of the fin or tail of the fish.

Piranha that hunt alone often trick other fish by pretending not to be interested and then attacking suddenly.

Young piranha have a unique hunting advantage. At a certain stage of early development, a juvenile piranha develops a distinctive marking near its tail. This makes the piranha look like some of the fish it preys on. The marking and the size of the piranha fool the other fish into thinking it is one of their own kind. The young piranha can swim freely among its prey, taking a bite out of whichever one is closest.

Piranha are always looking for their next meal, but the time of year influences how aggressively they will hunt and attack their prey. Piranha are at their most aggressive during the dry season.

Piranha and the Dry Season

South America has a tropical climate. This means that the temperature ranges from warm to hot. Therefore, rather than having four seasons, they have two: a wet season and a dry season. These seasons have a big effect on where piranha live and what they eat.

The rainy season begins suddenly with heavy rain, which lasts for about four months. During this time the lakes and rivers that the piranha live in flood into the flat, grassy plains that surround them. These floodplains, or **savannahs**, are home to a wide variety of animals. Birds, reptiles, amphibians, mammals, and fish all flourish during the rainy season.

The rain forests also flood during this time of year. As the rivers overflow their banks and flood the forest, many species of piranha feast on fruits and seeds that would not normally be available to them. The rainy season is a time when prey is easy to find. Piranha gen-

Water levels of the rivers and lakes of South America change dramatically throughout the year. Piranha struggle to survive during the dry season.

erally will not attack people or other large animals during this time because they are not starving or confined.

However, as the months pass, the rains gradually taper off until they stop altogether. Now the dry season begins. Without the rain to cool things down, the temperatures rise again. The floods recede as the hot sun dries the land. Many piranha do not make it back to the river in time. They find themselves in small ponds or lagoons. These trapped piranha quickly eat all the available food. Starving, with their environment shrinking more each day, this is the time when the piranha are the most ferocious. They will viciously attack anything that comes within their range.

Food During the Dry Season

Piranha are not the only ones struggling to survive during the dry season. As the days grow hotter, water becomes scarce. Larger animals soon find that the only watering holes available are teeming with starving piranha. Many animals have bites taken from their snouts or legs while trying to drink. An animal unlucky enough to fall into the water will be surrounded by piranha within seconds. The smell of its blood ex-

Starving piranha will attack any large animal that comes to the water for a drink.

cites the piranha into a feeding frenzy. Piranha may even jump out of the water to grab a chunk of flesh from the part of the animal that is still above the surface. Observers have noted that the water turns red with blood and seems to boil as the piranha dodge around, and sometimes inside, their victim. Often, when frantically attacking their prey, they accidentally bite each other. It is not unusual to see a piranha with a bite-sized hole in its back or side.

Young birds are also in danger of being eaten by piranha. Herons often build their nests in trees near the edge of a lagoon. Piranha gather under the branches of these trees and wait. They are frequently rewarded with a meal when a baby bird falls out of its nest into the water, or when a young heron fails in its attempts to learn to fly.

Although piranha can survive for over three months without food, many starve before the rains return. Others simply run out of oxygen as the lagoons they are trapped in dry into mere puddles on the plains. This makes them easy targets for predators.

CHAPTER FOUR

Killing the Killers: When Piranha Are Prey

Although piranha are fierce predators, they are not at the top of the food chain. A variety of other animals prey on piranha. Most of these are other animals that live in the lakes and rivers with the piranha. Other predators may be those that live near the banks of the river. Large predators can eat a small piranha in one bite. Smaller predators usually attack from behind to avoid the piranha's dangerous teeth. Piranha are most vulnerable to predators when they are young.

Piranha and Their Predators

Although young piranha are aggressive, they are also still very small and must spend a lot of their time hiding from predators. Even with their parents protecting them, many young piranha become prey to other

A caiman makes a meal of a piranha. Piranha are prey for a variety of animals including other fish, birds, dolphins, turtles, and otters.

fish, wading birds, or other animals that live in or near the water. Young piranha are often eaten by bigger species of piranha. They may even be eaten by their own parents, if other food cannot be found.

Since piranha lay so many eggs, baby piranha are an abundant source of food for other fish during the breeding season. These predators help to keep the piranha population under control. Adult piranha have fewer predators and need more food to survive. If too many piranha survive into adulthood they will have to compete with each other for food. This would result in piranha becoming even more ferocious in their attempts to survive and in many piranha starving to death.

Several animals prey on adult piranha. Smaller species may be eaten by birds, large-mouth catfish, peacock bass, and other fish. Larger species' predators include **caimans**, freshwater dolphins, turtles, otters, and large fish. Piranha are especially vulnerable toward the end of the dry season. By this time many of the lagoons have become little more than puddles. Deprived of food and oxygen, the piranha are too weak to fight back. They become easy prey for birds and animals that live near the water. The herons, whose babies they feasted on just a few weeks before, now feast on them.

People and Piranha

People often think that piranha prey on humans, but actually, the opposite is true. People fish for piranha

A red-bellied piranha hangs from a fish hook. Many people fish for piranha for food.

---

throughout South America. Piranha are considered to be a very good fish for eating. People who fish for piranha must be very careful. They use special wire fishing lines because the piranha can bite through ordinary lines. Fishermen who use nets may find that the piranha bite through them. Fishermen kill the piranha before they come into the boat. A live piranha will thrash around violently and take a chunk out of whatever comes within its range. Many people have been injured this way. People not only eat the meat of the piranha, but also use their jaws as tools.

South American Indians have used the jaws of the piranha for scissors and razors for thousands of years. Some native people wear the jaws on a string

To avoid being bitten, fisherman kill piranha before bringing them into the boat.

around their waist so that they can use them whenever the need arises. When these Indians saw scissors from Europe for the first time they called them "piranha." Some tribes still use the jaws for scissors today.

Piranha as Pests

Although people in South America have learned to live with piranha, some people still consider piranha to be pests. They make fishing difficult by biting through nets and lines or even eating parts of captured fish before they can be taken out of the water. Cattle herders worry that piranha will bite their cows when the cows drink or need to cross a river.

People have tried to get rid of piranha in several ways. They have put poison into the rivers and lakes where piranha live. This sometimes worked well for killing the piranha but it also killed many other kinds of fish living in the piranha habitat. Another problem with using poisons is that some piranha are naturally resistant to some poisons. These piranha survive to make babies that are also resistant, creating a population of piranha that cannot be killed with poison.

Other people have tried a more natural approach to get rid of piranha. They have put large numbers of piranha predators in the rivers where piranha live. Fish like peacock cichlids eat young piranha. People hope that by introducing these fish into the water they will eat the baby piranha before they reach adulthood, when they can cause a serious threat and are able to reproduce. Although this method has met with some success, it has also had a serious impact on the environment. With the peacock cichlids eating all the baby piranha, some of the fish native to the environment lose an important source of food. In addition, without the piranha scavenging for dead animals, these rivers are not as clean and healthy as they once were.

Piranha occupy an important **niche** in the ecosystem as scavengers and as prey for other animals. If people are successful in destroying them, the results will likely be damaging to the rivers, lakes, and surrounding areas.

The Future of the Piranha

Despite the efforts of people to eliminate them, the piranha's future looks bright. Piranha are tough and hardy fish. In addition, they are widespread throughout South America. Although some species inhabit only specific areas, no species is endangered. However, the piranha's environment is in danger.

Tropical rain forests are being cut down at alarming rates to make way for humans. As the rain forests disappear, piranha are forced into smaller spaces and have a harder time finding the seeds and fruits that they eat during the rainy season. In addition, human industries are polluting the rivers. Piranha can stand a good deal of pollution, but many of the animals they eat cannot. If their prey cannot live long enough to

Although many South Americans consider the piranha a pest, the fish play an essential role in the South American ecosystem.

reproduce, there could be serious food shortages for the piranha.

Scientists still have much to learn about piranha. They are difficult to study in the wild. But we do know that piranha are only dangerous to people in certain situations and that the piranha's role as scavengers makes them essential to the South American ecosystem.

NOTES

Chapter 1: The Legendary Piranha: Evil in the Amazon

1. Theodore Roosevelt, *Through the Brazilian Wilderness.* New York: Charles Scribner's Sons, 1914, pp. 42–43.

GLOSSARY

ambush: To suddenly attack after waiting in a hiding place.

caiman: An animal that is similar to an alligator and is native to South and Central America.

capybara: A large, semiaquatic rodent native to South America. Capybaras can reach up to four feet in length.

carnivore: An animal that eats only meat.

ecosystem: All the living things in an area and the way they affect each other and the environment.

fry: Recently hatched or juvenile fishes.

lateral line: A canal along the side of a fish, containing pores that open into tubes supplied with sense organs sensitive to low vibrations.

niche: The ecological role of an organism in a community, especially in regard to food consumption.

omnivore: An animal that is able to eat both plants and meat.

savannah: A tropical grassland containing scattered trees and drought-resistant undergrowth.

scavenger: An animal that eats dead or decaying matter.

shoal: A large number of fish swimming as a group.

spawn: To produce eggs.

Weberian apparatus: The first four vertebrae of a piranha's backbone, which connect to the inner ear and enhance the piranha's hearing.

FOR FURTHER EXPLORATION

Books

Mary Berendes, *Piranhas*. Chanhassen, MN: Child's World, 1999. This is a short book with some good color pictures and basic information about piranha.

Susan Grossman, *Piranhas*. New York: Dillon, 1994. This book has information about piranha and wonderful color photographs. There is also a map of the piranha's range and an excellent glossary.

Emily McAuliffe, *Piranhas*. New York: Capstone, 1998. This book contains information about piranha, including their habits, life cycle, and different kinds of piranha. Also includes a fast facts section and an excellent photo diagram of a piranha.

John R. Quinn, *Piranhas: Fact and Fiction*. Neptune City, NJ: T.F.H. Publications, 1992. This is primarily a how-to book for people who want to keep piranha as pets. However, it does have some good information and a gallery of species, which features both photos and drawn illustrations of piranha.

Websites

Enchanted Learning (www.enchantedlearning.com). This site has a labeled printout of the parts of a piranha to color, as well as a few piranha facts.

Extreme Science (www.extremescience.com). This website focuses on the ferocious nature of piranha. There is a good picture of a piranha's mouth and some good basic information.

Frank Magallanes, Oregon Piranha and Exotic Fish Exhibit (www.angelfire.com/biz/piranha038/index.html). The archives of this website offer a great deal of information about piranha. Of special interest is a reproduction of an article from *National Geographic* called "Seeking the Truth About the Feared Piranha."

INDEX

PICTURE CREDITS

ABOUT THE AUTHOR

Rachel Lynette has never been bitten by a piranha. She has taught writing and computer applications courses for children of all ages, and she has also worked as a teacher for the Pacific Science Center in Seattle. Lynette received her B.A. in Psychology from Western Washington University and is currently working on her master's degree. Her articles on children and family life have appeared in *Seattle Child* and *Northwest Baby and Child*. Lynette lives in the Songaia Cohousing Community with her husband, Scott, and their children, David and Lucy.